What
Kind of
Woman

What Kind of Woman

Poems

Kate Baer

ORION
SPRING

First published in the United States in 2020 by Harper Perennial

First published in Great Britain in 2021 by Orion Spring
an imprint of The Orion Publishing Group Ltd
Carmelite House, 50 Victoria Embankment
London EC4Y 0DZ

An Hachette UK Company

3 5 7 9 10 8 6 4

A CIP catalogue record for this book is
available from the British Library.

Designed by Jen Overstreet

ISBN (Hardback) 978 1 3987 0682 8
ISBN (eBook) 978 1 3987 0684 2

Printed in Great Britain by Clays Ltd, Elcograf S.p.A.

ORION
SPRING

www.orionbooks.co.uk

For my teachers

What
Kind of
Woman

Part I

Advice for Former Selves

Burn your speeches, your instructions,
your prophecies too. In the morning when
you wake: stretch. Do not complain. Do not
set sail on someone else's becoming, their voice
in your throat. Do not look down your nose
at a dinner party, laughing: *If only they didn't
have so many children.*

Revision is necessary. The compulsory bloom.
When you emerge with crystals in one hand,
revenge in the other, remember the humble
barn swallow who returns in spring. If not
for her markings, another bird entirely.

Ego

I once had a boyfriend who would not let me
watch him eat. He did not want me to see him
grind and swallow, gulp and guzzle, suck the
marrow from his teeth.

He did not want me to see him need.

Not Like Other Girls

Not with that loose demeanor, your
chilled-out tone, the way you do not
care if he does or does not call. You can
keep up. Speak with self-assurance. Run
with the best of them. You are what we call
a *sweet enigma*, all dreams and bottle caps.
No lisp of weakness on your tongue.

No, you're not like other girls, he says,
beaming. Praise for all you've left behind.

Twenties

I found my first gray hair at nineteen, slept with her son at twenty-one. For months I ate nothing but beans and cotton balls. For years I did nothing but yawn. I will never be as young as the night I put on a long red dress and danced in the street with you. Some things we don't remember; some things will always taste the same. First— the thrill of fast cigarettes. Second—the significance of *signs*. Once I kissed a girl in Jerusalem, all legs and cherry lips. I did not take her number. I did not know how much I'd long to hold her in my arms again.

College Boy

You brought wine and a grin that said
most beautiful girl. And I drank while
you watched (while you sat there and
watched) my whole mouth turn to slurs,
to a slick open wound. To a place for
your unraveling.

(Did you know when you bait a deer
it's called a *violation*, but when you poison
a girl it's called a *date*.)

My roommate watched while you
carried me, limp and sleeping, up
carpet stairs.

(What if this is what I wanted?)

In the morning, you asked if I was
sleeping. As if my clothes still held
me. As if I'd ever been awake.

First Love

You were the Eden of my youth. All
sand and sun, cerulean eyes. A paradise
with limbs. Together we went climbing
on the edge of rocks (on the edge of any
thing).

Do you remember my sister's laugh? The
Chevy's smell? The way we cried when they
pulled his body from the waves?

Sometimes I imagine what it'd be like to
show you I'm alive. The thrill of it. The sharp
inhale. The nerve exposed. The bone.

Girls' Night Out

In restaurants we argue over who will
pay even though the real question is
who will confess their children are dull
or their marriage has holes at the knees.
We order french fries, salads, and brie.
Hold wine to our lips. Pull truth from
our bags that we kept all along.

She wonders—do you remember when
I cried in the cab. Wore that shirt with
the sleeves. Left him alone in the rain.

We do, we do.

Moon Song

You are not an evergreen, unchanged
by the pitiless snow. You are not a photo,
a brand, a character written for sex or
house or show. You do not have to choose
one or the other: a dream or a dreamer, the
bird or the birder. You may be a woman of
commotion and quiet. Magic and brain.

You can be a mother and a poet. A wife and
a lover. You can dance on the graves you dug
on Tuesday, pulling out the bones of yourself
you began to miss. You can be the sun and the
moon. The dance a victory song.

Backyard Wedding

Nobody is looking at you, my girlfriend says
when I ask if I can wear my yellow dress to a
backyard wedding. But that is not the point
of yellow dresses or backyard weddings or the
pairs of father-sons with all their suffering. I
could name each one if you like. Johns and
Mikes and Robs and Deans and other names
that sound the same. *But not my John*,
she'd say, hands at her throat. Oh no—

not yours. He's a real family man. Head on
his shoulders. Nice kind of guy. I did meet a
John once who'd call me on Sundays and tell
me all the ways women had disappointed him:
thin hair, small breasts, dirt under the finger-
nails. *Which one am I?* I asked one night
awake on the phone. He laughed as if I did
not know. As if I could not see my own face.

Plot Lines for Female Leads

She was a slip of a girl. Slender and
long. The most delicate hands. Angular
jaw. Lean like a deer. Moved like a swan.
Unbuttered toast was the only thing she
ate all day.

My Friend Bethany Rages
at the News

A Beautiful Celebrity Woman is asked: what is your
beauty secret? She answers: *hot lemon water every
morning*. She does not answer: *time*. She does not say
the names of every woman who scrubs her bathroom tile
and carries children to and from the car.

A child is shot at a convenience store. An expert's asked:
what is the derivation? He answers: *parents and video
games*. He does not answer: *guns*. He does not mention
gross convenience. He does not say how an angry man
can buy several killing machines.

A young girl tries to save the earth. An online post asks:
what is her importance? A man answers: *she is nothing but
an ugly whore*. He does not answer: *I am lonely*.
He does not say how every time they show her face, all he
sees is every girl who has taken her love away.

Female Candidate

I like her but / aggressive tone / it's not that she / now that I have
daughters / if only she would / in that short haircut / nothing against
the way she dresses / if she wasn't a baby killer / I don't know how he
could marry / how she can stand up in those shoes / with a child in
school / here comes the feminism / not enough / warmth is important /
no class is the problem and / anti-woman is the word I would use / not
American if she doesn't / give glory to / show some leg / I cannot vote
for the kind of woman who / has a stick up her / not my kind of girl

Dearly Beloved

I write eulogies for my friends, brief and
beautiful. I will write one for you too—
driving down the highway or in the shower or
given the chance for a long city walk. I will begin,
"She was one of the good ones," then pause for the
tremors of grief.

I got engaged when I was eighteen to a boy I would never
marry. I loved him more than anyone has ever loved,
and still I cut him open, held his heart to his throat.
(When I am buried, tell him that the only thing I meant
to do was *live*.)

Death is a funny thing, but I won't say that on the day
you die. Instead I will pull on my long black clothes and
give my words to you.

It's Like This

Mary Ruefle used the word *snail* in two poems so that I could use the word *grief* in all of mine. The problem is we all want to see a little suffering: dead mothers, bad fathers, the redbird crushed beneath the wheel. All the days we've lived through, we just want to say, at least it wasn't me.

Fat Girl

Hard to describe / I don't know how to say / great person-
ality / real pretty face but / the heavier type of / low self-esteem
and / I don't know if she's thought of / program to cut carbs /
friend has a sister who / lost all the weight but / it's hard for
some people / I want her to be healthy / I can't imagine / biggest
she's been in / long time since I've seen her / I know it's a battle /
I know how she struggles / to let herself go

To Take Back a Life

First, you must learn desire. Hold its
fruit in your hands. Unmarry it from
the hunger to be held, to be wanted, to
be called from the streets like the family
dog. You are not a *good girl*. You are not
somebody's otherness. This is not a dress
rehearsal before a better kind of life.

Pick up your heavy burdens and leave
them at the gate. I will hold the door for
you.

Things My Girlfriends Teach Me

When in doubt, *try it on*. Keep it simple.
Don't waste time worrying if they will see
you from behind. No one on this entire
earth cares more about your life than you.

Eat a breakfast. Find a God. Make a casserole
to freeze. If you're walking on a deserted road,
send me your location. Remember you don't
need a straw.

Drink more water. Fold your sweaters. This
is the time to buy a hat. When life throws
you a bag of sorrow, hold out your hands.

Little by little, mountains are climbed.

Nothing Tastes as Good as Skinny Feels

Unless you count your grandmother's
cake, hand mixed while she waits for the
sound of your breath at the door. Or if
you consider the taste of the sea, arms
raised while you enter, salt at your lips.
Or maybe you've forgotten the taste of
a lover, your mouth on his skin. I ask—

have you ever tasted the cool swill of
freedom? The consuming rush of a
quiet, radical love.

Unsettling

Masked teller.
Masked shopper.
Masked baby.
Masked butcher.
Masked runner.
Masked neighbor.
Masked lover.
Masked wife.

Robyn Hood

Imagine if we took back our diets,
our grand delusions, the time spent
thinking about the curve of our form.
Imagine if we took back every time we
called attention to one or the other: her
body, our body, the bad shape of things.

Imagine the minutes that would stretch
into hours. Day after day stolen back like
a thief.

Imagine the power of loose arms and
assurance. The years welcomed home
in a soft, cotton dress.

The Women Who Walk Us Home

The ones who arrive with a bag of clothes, four
tired lemons, half a story from her sister's trip to

Paraguay. The ones who keep our secrets and whose
secrets we keep in potted plants, in every ocean we've

ever known. The ones who know our husbands, their
little pleasures. Our lovers and our scars. The ones

who stay, hope like a moth. Who stare into the gaping
tomb and are not afraid of its unveiling. The ones who

will be there, even then (even then), to walk us home.

Things Men Say to Me

Fun fact! You will like this. Fun fact!
I knew your mother before you were born.
Fun fact! I don't normally read women writers
but I have read you. Explain to me your angle.
Tell me why you're so mad about *men*. You seem
like the kind of person who appreciates a story.
This is just my opinion. These are just some things
I have been meaning to write down. Give me your
ideas. Give me something fun to talk about. Let me
tell you all the ways I see a girl like you.

2020

we complain about the price of coffee
as if it isn't becoming extinct
along with the rest of us
would it be so wrong if we cut off
every billionaire at the knees
would it be so wrong if
I touched my face to yours
two men run for office
it doesn't matter who they've ruined
this is the year I unfriend
anyone who uses a beauty filter
who fetishizes youth into social currency
I don't know
how someone can write about southern roots
who lives in Massachusetts
I don't know
how we manage our ordinary lives
when we're this close to the death in dying
go ahead and tell me otherwise
go ahead and tell me something good

Comment Section

for Karen

I wish you would <mark>stick to poetry</mark>
<mark>instead of constantly being</mark>
<mark>political, just one reader preference</mark>

<mark>have you ever thought what</mark>
<mark>would happen if the police</mark>
disappear <mark>ed?</mark>

is what you say <mark>going to change</mark>
<mark>anything? (No)</mark>

when you stay <mark>in your lane,</mark>
<mark>better connection happens</mark>

<mark>I know staying</mark> silent <mark>isn't cool</mark>
<mark>but just a thought</mark>

In Lieu of a Thank You Card

Send me your distractions. Your pity laugh,
the auburn couch, the way you pull your hair
into tiny thimbles of grief.

I will take your conversations too—the one you
had with your mother on a Saturday. Or every
time you stood inside a door to weep.

The best thanks is the sound of your heart
beating. Your hands soaring above the waves.

When Uncle Brian Asks If We Sit Around and Burn Bras

We gather as we always have: Naomi and
Ruth, Aphrodite and Helen, Eve and her
lioness. We are good girls. Mothers and
dancers and counselors. We are wicked
too, but we won't tell you this. Instead
we arrange plates of bread and fruit, slip
into the center of each other. Find our
childhoods, our varied pleasures, the aged
and blistered scars.

We are half drunk, half destroyed. Nothing
left but blood and bone. Still we surface—
fold into each other like paper cranes. Her,
like a long-lost lover. Her, a cool and
healing balm.

Commencement Address

When I take my evening walk, I unlock rooms
I never meant to close, which is one way

to write a book. Another is to peel
an orange or take a shower or

fall in love with someone dangerous.

At any given moment there is someone getting
what they always wanted.

I know no quicker way to ruin a day
than to dwell on this.

Some Nights

Some nights she walks out to the
driveway where the lilacs bloom and
lies down on the warm pavement even
though the neighbors will see and wonder
what kind of woman does such things.

There she stares up at the slender moon
and thinks about the baby albatross filled
with discarded spoons or the time a friend
asked what she was working on these days
and she answered, "Who has the time?"
even though she meant something else
entirely.

Across the lawn the crickets sing while the
earth lets out its tired breath and wanders
through the trees to greet her.

Part II

Like a Wife

The week before my wedding, my friend's dad said:
just don't get fat, like other wives do.

And so I brined him in a deep salt bath, added thyme
and celery. Devoured him whole, in one big bite,
so he could see just how hungry a woman can be.

Curveball

This is a love story, Phoebe Waller-Bridge
wrote. Though in fairness they always are.
Even when it is imagined. Even when it ends
with the shower running, towel at your waist.
Even when the last thing you say is, *I never liked
your mother anyway*.

When I took you as a husband I did not know
the deaths our love would suffer. I did not know
the graves of loneliness. Last week when you asked
if I ever thought of leaving, I said *no*, even though
what I meant was that I love the feel of your hands
in the morning. That even in our darkest hours,
I still wait for the sound of your feet at the door.

For the Advice Cards at Bridal Showers

Go to bed angry. Wake up with a plan. When
someone asks for the secret to a happy marriage,
remember you don't know. This is not a happy
ending. This is not a *fairy tale*. This is the beginning
of a life you haven't met. It doesn't matter how much
you fall down on your knees, brown the buttered pan—
time will reveal love's complication. Gloom and
happiness.

For now just remember how you felt the day you
were born: desperate for magic, ready to love.

What I Meant

What I meant when I said "I don't have time" is that
every minute that passes I'm disappointing someone
and
what I meant when I said "leaving is harder than you think" is that
there's only one other person who cares as much about your son as you
and
what I meant when I said "you'll see someday" is that
there will come a time when you can no longer stomach the sound
of everybody singing "Happy Birthday"
and
what I meant when I said "I haven't really been reading" is that
sometimes I imagine what it would be like to fall asleep on a moving
train and wake up on the other side

Hot Meals, Biology

My husband does not like poetry. The
soft, ambling words with no beginning
or strong, reliable end. Instead he likes
more certain things: hot meals, biology,
the feel of the putting green.

What he doesn't know is how much the
touch of his baby's skin or the way his
mother forms his favorite pie, thinking
about the morning he was born, is all a
verse. A covert melody.

Deleted Sentences

Dear husband. Dear lover. Dear darling of my heart. No, I do not want to attend the barbecue scheduled cruelly over naptime. I do not want to go to the recital either. Can you tell your sister that too? In the morning I saw you dancing with our daughter and for a moment I almost cried. I hate when people say *I almost cried*. Why even mention it at all?

What time will you be home? What time do you think you may be home? What time should we wait for you outside on the lawn while the pasta boils over and the baby cries because he misses you? Oh, before I go—what time will you be home?

Sometimes I wonder what would happen if you died and I had to write a eulogy while lost in my grief. What would I say? And who would take out the trash bins on dark Sunday nights or hold our children while they cried through fever dreams?

What time will you be home?

What Kind of Woman

Wedlock

Here we are in the belly of it. First the mornings,
clipped and broken, followed by the evening and,
at times, an afternoon. Where are you when I call
you from the top of the stairs? Where are you when
I ask how funny it is that so-and-so went and did
those things you said you'd never do? Come closer
so I can see that you are listening. Move farther so
I can sleep away from all that breath and sound.

In the yard we are sunshine and hydrangea. In the
house we are nothing but time; the bedside table,
the chest of drawers, the grandfather clock you
found along the road. The children revolve through
our doorways like planets. We ask: *Is it true he left
her for another? Is it true she never loved him anyway?*

Some nights we move together like two desperate
creatures. Some nights we roll apart like two tired
wives. We ask: *Is it true you can be one thing then
another? Is it true you can be loved anyway?*

One Thousand Wives

The secret is my husband has many wives.
One for bluebird mornings, one for doubt
in the afternoon. One for the stretch of
evening when the children perform their
endless rituals. There is the *business* wife.
The *wanting* wife. The wife who stands
on the front porch and needs to *talk to you*.

For a time we have the good wife. The *thin*
wife. Eventually the dead wife. The ghost
of every woman who tried to change for
you.

What Kind of Man

What kind of man weeps at the feet
of his wife in pain, holds up the pink
and shrieking thing and feels the throb
of time. What kind of man wraps a cloth
around his waist and holds the baby to
his chest, walks through the streets swaying
like a drunk in morning. What kind of man
feels the rage of men and only swallows at
his daughter's fists at his chest. What kind
of man does not give up his time, his many
pleasures, but hands them over without a
sound. What kind of man bends to hold
them in their suffering, in their questions,
in their garbled turns of phrase. What kind
of man admits his failures, turns over his
heavy stones, stands at the feet of grief and
wanting and does not turn away. What kind
of man becomes a father. A lasting place.
A steady ship inside a tireless storm.

Ode to My Desire

I have always been hungry; fingers dipped
in sugar, salt across my lips. Four children
have passed through my body and still here
I am, asking for your hands on my hips,
voice in my ear. For melon and honey cream.
For you to not make love to me. Take me—

but wait until I plead. There is nothing like
the impatient thrum of wanting. All legs
and foaming mouth.

In hallways I play a game called "kissing,"
imagining every woman as a lover, every man
with his mouth on mine. How different
they must look when they are in heat.

Fresh Lemonade

Justin gets a real kick out of his wife's
lemonade. *She makes it from scratch*,
he says. Not like other wives with their
short haircuts and pale linen suits. *Not*

that there's anything wrong with that, he
grins. And look: the gal on my block, she
gets up at four to care for the dying and my
cousin on 3rd teaches the kids in the south

part of town. We need women like them,
a real motherly touch. *Oh yeah*, they agree.
Roger says his wife is too busy to work,
what with the boys and their schedules

and large appetites. *Can you believe how
much they eat in one sitting?* he laughs,
never having made a meal big enough
to fill more than his plate.

Missed Connections

I was trying on my wedding dress fifteen years later, and you came in
and said *why on earth did you keep that old thing?*

You were ducking out the door in a hurry and turned to say
I love you in that color, but I had already left to drink my morning tea.

All day I felt the rush of sex, the feeling of your hands between my
thighs, but when I bent to kiss your neck, you said, *I have some indigestion.*

You turned over in the black of night and took my hand against
your chest, but all I wanted was the warmth of my own blanket. All I
could dream of was sleep.

Marriage as a Death

In the beginning, a spectacle. A
ceremony bearing witness. Greeters
down the aisles, flowers on their coats.
Only later does it hang off our shoulders
with its gray dust. *Forever* sitting on our
doorstep while others pay tribute. *How
long has it been?* Ten years. Fifteen years.
Twenty-some and counting.

We haunt ourselves in passing. You still
here? I'm here, too.

During This Double Date We Will Prove We Have a Happy Marriage

The problem is we're running late and your shirt is wrong—like a dried-up tangerine. I say, I hate to keep them waiting. When really I mean, I'd rather pull my hair out than be in the car with you. This wasn't your idea. This isn't your *cup of tea*. So instead of fingering the necklace around my neck, you stare down at your shoes. I'm thinking about your mother. I'm thinking about my jeans. I'm thinking about the time you answered, *I liked the other pair*. I want you to be funny. I want you to be loose. I want you to walk into the restaurant and say, *everything is true*. I am a giving husband. This is my lover wife. We have a happy marriage. There is nothing in this world I'd rather do than share a meal with you.

Etymology of the Word *Wife*

from the Indo-European root, ghwibh,
which means pudenda or *shame*

shame from the Old English, scamu,
which means modesty or *private part*

private from the Latin word privatus,
which means personal or *peculiar*

peculiar from the mid-fifteenth-century
meaning "belonging exclusively to one
person" or *private property*

Crescendo

The moment in the argument
when the only sound between us
is the buzz of locusts, cars from a
passing street, God licking her
fingertips, wondering how this is
going to go.

Vow Renewal

I ask my husband to tell me he likes
thick thighs and he says yes he does,
though he stammers and stalls.

My friend Rhoda asks her husband if
she should go back to school to be a singer
and he says, *I've never even heard you sing*.

My friend Colleen calls her husband on
a Friday and says this is the last time she
will make his dinner. And he says, well—

My friend Kristy tells her husband she
is not his mother, and he cries because all
this time, he didn't know.

Marriage Tales

After arguments they speak through emails.
Dear Wife, I'm sorry I insulted the ravioli and
Dear Husband, I'm sorry you did not write down
the appointment we spoke of on Tuesday.

In bed they sleep like corpses until the morning,
when the children sing a resurrection song. First
one, then another. Damp in their footed pajamas,
hands at her shirt.

On weekends they drive to the country to talk
about traffic and look down into the brown lake
where the baby almost drowned. There they eat
sandwiches and he gives her pearl earrings and a
card to say *thank you* for surrendering her body
to the cause.

In return she gives it up again and again, laughing
at the pleasure, the audacity, the ambition of it all.

On Our Anniversary

There is no white and layered cake to
thaw. No dinner on a sunlit balcony.
Instead there is only the belly of time.
Card games, city blocks, the heirloom
tomatoes brought in before the storm.

Who are you without our daughter's
laugh? Without their bodies asleep
in our bed?

Why You Shouldn't Marry Me

I was born in another state
like it is something special
to have more than one city.
When someone says some-.
thing strange about a party,
I assume it's a surprise party
just for me. In another life
I was a dancer: black eyes,
sharp teeth, the kind of
mouth to make your mother
scream. I can be beautiful
if I want to. I can take your
rabbit ears and disappear
them with my tongue. If
you listen, I will tell you all
the ways I have betrayed you.
Line them up, secure the
edges, turn them into stars.

When I Ask My Grandmother Why She Let Him Come Back Home

There is so much more to love.
I would have missed it—
the ducks and chickens, children calling
from the yard. The way he'd say *you are so*
beautiful. One cannot complete the other.
One cannot hold on to brokenness.
The cruel things we could have done—

I would have missed the ball games. His
eyes searching across a swarming table,
the thrill of spring and heavy snow.

Think about it—every wedding, every
Sunday, every light strung across the living
room.

I would have missed all this.

Fear of Happiness

Sometimes I wonder how fast we could pack the car in the event of the world ending. I make a list of things we'd need: rubber gloves, jars of fruit and honey, cloths for the baby's bottom. I think about where we'd go—land with fields and sheds and massive gardens. To a place with god and loaded guns. I think about the nights, how we'd sleep in a row of breathing bodies. How we'd marry each day as it comes.

Observations Through the Glass at the Human Zoo

You'll notice the female at home with her young.
This is the time of pacing, four thirty in the afternoon.
Sighs and mottled cries. For dinner she prepares beans
and butter rice. You see her satisfaction. You see her lick
her lips when she tastes the cheese and sour cream.
Outside, the male approaches slowly. See how he
scoops up his offspring. See how she turns when he
tries to touch her cheek.

Now is what they call the evening. We do not know
why she waits on the stairs to listen. Why she smiles
into her hands.

Little Miracles

To end up in this home with its red
front door and casual crumbling. To
fill it with sunlamps and paper chains.
To hear the thud of children, songs at
their lips. To unclasp the thought of
leaving, tie it to the door. To run into
the gaping mouth of change and know
its suffering.

To find the ones who say, *I am not
afraid of sitting in the dark with you.*

After a Psychic Tells Me I'm Going to Die

I'll plant a garden full of colored pebbles.
In the evening when the dew breaks, I'll
kneel down in the slick grass and pray for
every man who gave himself to greed. I'll do
the dishes, scrub grit from dirty pans, tell
my mother, *you did the best you could.* I'll
go back to college, pay off my sister's debts.
Swallow every hair instead of leaving them
on the ground. When I dream of snakes who
call me *baby*, I'll wake my husband just to tell
him how much he shines. I'll be polite. Torch
every *shit* and *pisses.* Give away my books and
little screens. I'll be good. I'll be the wife and
keeper. I'll do anything just to live.

Part III

Part III

Third Trimester

She walks, though gravity does its part
to slow her. The heavy pull between her

knees, the low and aching strain. She walks
through vineyards, by city malls, down the

streets of her hometown. She walks and
walks and walks until she stops to hold the

bulb of herself, take in the dulled landscape
(the blackbird's call, the greening picket fence).

Who are you when the sum of your being
grows beyond your private mind? She walks

to answer even though she knows she is an
ocean, a vital pulse, the oldest truest song.

For the Advice Cards at Baby Showers

Baby socks don't matter, but more importantly—
neither does advice. This is not a performance
for your friend or your mother or the woman
in line who tells you about *coats*. Experience will
teach you two things: you are the mother and it's
okay to let them go up the slide. Nothing in this
world can prepare you for this love's suffering. For
joy and loneliness.

For now just remember: birds sing, babies cry,
and no matter the weather, every morning is new.

Deliverance

You are born in the morning, sunlight
blazing against the sharp gasp of labor.
In an instant you arrive, loud and longing.
Look, your father says. A soppy miracle.

What is the word for when the light leaves
the body? What is the word for when it, at
last, returns?

New Year

Look at it, cold and wet like a newborn
calf. I want to tell it everything—how we
struggled, how we tore out our hair and
thumbed through rusted nails just to
stand for its birth. I want to say: *look how
far we've come*. Promise our resolutions.

But what does a baby care for oaths and
pledges? It only wants to live.

Motherload

She keeps an office in her sternum, the flat
bone in the center of her chest with all its
urgent papers, vast appointments, lists of
minor things. In her vertebrae she holds more
carnal tasks: milk jugs, rotten plants, heavy-
bottomed toddlers in all their mortal rage.

She keeps frustration in her hallux: senseless
chatter, jealous fangs, the spikes of a dinosaur's
tail. The belly is more complicated—all heartache
and ambition. Fires and tidal waves.

In her pelvis she holds her labors, long and
slippery. In her clavicle, silent things. (Money
and power. Safety and choice. Tiny banquets
of shame.)

In her hands she carries their egos, small and
flimsy. In her mouth she holds their laughter,
gentle currents, a cosmos of everything.

Social Studies

The night the baby died in her father's arms
trying to cross an ocean, our children slept.
It is easy to list off platitudes. To write down
every time we cupped a spider in our hands
and let it out the door. There are many poems
about the seasons, less about the time it takes
to bury another child. It's true—

history has taught us to be good to children,
to treat the earth as a living place. To stand on
the side of every man and every woman who
begs to land in the same green grass as you.

First Woman

First woman, then mother. Heart-eyed and
weak-kneed in the pale nursery light. Hold
your tender battle wounds and be baptized
in the cold slant of rain against the shopping
cart. There is no time for crying now (one is
already enough).

Where do we go when the beams of our ship
have rotted? When every word comes out in
our mother tongue? There is no room for
company among the weeping, among the
sour apples and milk-drenched things. *Isn't
this what you always wanted?*

Then one day on the street she calls to you.
First: *hello*. Second: *oh yes*. In your kitchen
she finds some water, holds the baby to her
chest. She might as well be nursing him. In
time she is no different from another limb.

Fortune Telling

Even though I still have my own
young children, even though they
rake my body over until it's limp
with decay, even though I cannot
bear the sound of another child
calling for his mother—I know I
will be one of those old women
who walks up to your family and
says: *look, you are so beautiful.*

Interview with Self

Can I have it all?

No.

Can I have it all?

No.

Can I have it all?

No.

Mary's Disappearance

Someone keeps stealing Mary. First from the porcelain set bought on a holiday, then in roadside nativity scenes. She has been removed, disappeared from the mall's store window, the church's glass, Aunt Miriam's table set. Have you noticed, I say to anyone who will listen, that all the Marys are gone? No one answers or tries to listen (*let's not talk politics*). My nephew's plastic set sits above the fireplace. Where is the mother? I ask, turning over every figurine. But the wisemen keep their silence, begging us to ask if, in fact, she ran.

Transfiguration

I dreamt myself into a mother,
but when I became her, I had to
dream her back into a woman
back into a woman
back into a woman
again.

Good Mother

She lies on her back, open shirt like a
wound, and waits for the start of her
baby crying. (What is it about the sound?
A symphony of doubt.) She walked into
motherhood in the low light of morning.
Now she sits at its feet in the dark and
weeps. *You are a good mother*, they say,
blood at her breast. *But what*, she asks,
does a good mother do?

Outside in the garden she pulls at the
thistles and dandelion weeds. Any sign
of failing. Any sign of immorality.

What Children Say

I can't reach my cup, my water bottle,
the snack up on the shelf. I can't do
it. I won't do it. I would never do it
in a million years. You need to help
me. Help me faster. Do it the way
I asked you to. I don't like pizza or
watermelon. I don't like anything I
liked before. I do not want it. I do
not need it. I will never move up off
this floor. Do not help me. Do not
hold me. Do not sit down beside my
bed. I'm not sleeping. I'm not tired.
I'm too scared to fall asleep. You must
hold me. You must rock me. Do not
leave me all alone. I am thirsty. I am
hungry. I am too tired to put my toys
away. Do not be angry. Do not start
singing. Where is the butterfly I drew?
I'm still hungry. I'm still playing. Will
you leave me? Will you stay?

Childhood

I do not remember being born
or how I knew my mother's face.
Only that we woke to the sound
of pots banging against the stove,
knowing she would be downstairs.

Dogs at the Park

I am aware of dogs at the park. I am
aware of men too. The number of
steps to the keys, to the car, to the long
stretch of grass where the baby lolls to
and fro, sticks in his teeth. They ask—
what good is a life with fear at your edges?
And I ask—what mother does not listen
to the slam of the sedan door and turn
to see what ghost emerges? We are the
gatekeepers, the sentinels. Maybe he is
just a man walking or maybe he is
searching for a bird to break. How
many have already been broken? Let
us count their wings.

If My Daughter Wrote a Poem

My mother squats in linen overalls and
complains about her knees. *It is like Christmas
morning*, she says when the basil blooms and
the tomatoes hang heavy on the vine. My mother
used to be beautiful. My mother used to be thin.
My mother used to carry us in baby carriers
against her chest until our bodies would go
limp with sleep.

Sometimes my mother roars, rage like a tooth.
Sometimes there is nothing to try but time.

Here is my mother sleeping. Look at the way
her lips are parted. Look at the way she can finally
close her eyes.

My son

cries because he's thinking about the length
of heaven. He asks—*how long does forever feel?*

My son,
my heart outside my body.

I don't know, I say.

I don't know.
I don't know.
I don't know.

Back to School Shopping

Because I love you, I buy the Superman backpack,
three tubs of glue. I hold up the different folders and
let you decide: tigers or LEGOs, stripes or battleships.
I do not tell you what I am becoming. I do not tell you
I am afraid. Last night they played the screams of some
people dying. Last night they showed their guns in the
air. How does a mother hold her terrors? How does
a school become a haunted place?

In the morning, I take your picture in front of the sign,
gaps in your teeth. I do not say a life without you is not
worth living. I do not say I've memorized every inch of
your frame. Instead, I wave at your hand waving.
Instead, I say a quick goodbye.

Bus Stop

My son asks me to stop saying
I love you at the bus stop. No kissing
either; even a side-hug is vaguely forbidden.

Against my better judgment,
I remind him from where he came.
I say—*I carried you in my womb.*
I held you every day
until you were born.

But he only shrugs.

Says, *I didn't ask you to.*

Mother's Mind

I count the deaths at each transition: three lost
on the way to the grocery store, four on a trip
to the creek. What if no one watches the mower
mowing? What if no one sees his body move
across the street? I am one step ahead of howling,
one breath shy of grief. Take my hands and reveal
the living. Rip the seam out of the story sewn. It is
one thing to imagine (it is another to walk among
the graves). At night I tuck my dread into the covers,
check its pulse before the dawn.

You ask: how can I keep this tired practice? I ask:
how can I leave this haunting place?

On the Floor of the Family Car

Here lies all the underbrush, discarded
clues to matters held outside the metal
hull (a contact lens, a stuffed jaguar, a
smear of dirt from a past ball game).

Who has left a fast food wrapper
stuffed under the driver's seat?
And who had thought it wise to
leave without a shoe?

(A clarinet, a dried earthworm, a bag
of grapes pressed down to make a rich
and redolent wine.)

Things No One Says to Me

You make it look so easy
You don't look like you just had a baby
Motherhood looks good on you

Stronger That You Know

My friend's young daughter tells her mother:
you're stronger that you know.
We repeat this, even though it doesn't make
sense. We say it to cheer each other up. We
say it, knowing how much harder it is: *that* vs.
than. One suggests it was always inside you.
The other suggests it's better you've learned
the coin can flip either way.

We tell our daughters they can be anything.
We call them *warrior, fierce,* and *brave*
as if they arrive in war paint and heels
to fight off our old demons.

And when they suffer, which they do,
we offer our consolations:

This is a part of it.
Take a deep breath.
Look at you kicking your legs.

On the Evening of Her Birth

On the evening of her birth, the first one with
its dim light and tender room, an afterbirth
still pulsing.

Here is the beginning, the earth and its fragility
heaped on your chest while you lean over to drink,
still clad in the robe you picked out with your mother
one Saturday. Even the glass of water is poetry now.

There is a shriek of hunger, your bruised body bending.
Oh, you wonder, *is this religion?* The swirl of hair tucked
under your chin while you breathe:

I am yours, I am yours, I am yours.

The Martian

Take my hand, this is what we call *the world*.
Sometimes we call it *the earth*, the most gentle
of words. Other times, *a heaping pile of shit*.
These are people. Those are trees. That is how
we move across the fields (it is called a *train*).
This is my eyelash, that is my cheek, the sound
you just heard is called a *sneeze*. Observe the
creatures moving across the floor: *ant, spider,
cat, child* (you may only smash the smallest of
these). Here are my pencils, this is my coat. In
the winter, frozen water falls from the sky (this
is what we call *snow*). That is a button. This is
a breeze. In the trash we have an assortment of
things (blood and paper, peels and plastic
strings.)

That is a cello. This is a mosque. The shouting
outside is what we call *fear*. If we hurry we will
find a *sunset*. If we slow we can find *ice cream*.
That is a candle. This is a door. Here is the light
it carries. Here is the comfort it brings.

What Mothers Say

I am tired. I am sleeping. I am heading
up to bed. Is it Tuesday? What's to-
morrow? When's the last I slept alone?
I am thinking. I am talking. Do you see
I'm on the phone? Bring the dishes, find
your blanket, put that book back on the
shelf. It is bedtime. It is rest time. You
need to go and brush again. I am working.
I am eating. This is why we bought you
toys. Go and play now, find your brother,
find elsewhere to make your ship. I am
angry, you're not listening. Please stop
crying on the floor. It's a school night.
Do your homework. Let me come and
scratch your back. I am listening. I can
hear you. Thanks for telling me the
truth. Let me closer, let me help you.
I am here now. Let me stay.

Body Back

In labor she is untamed. Body arching against the pain,
bright and cutting, until at last the smell of earth and blood.
Oh! she cries. A velvet scalp arrives under her chin. *Oh.*

At home she is a deflated balloon. Bruised fruit. All hips and skin
and breasts. She cradles herself in one arm, babe in the other.
To the doctor: should she still be limping to and from the car?

A woman on the screen says she's getting her body back. From
where, she does not know. Once, she pulls on jeans, dark and fitted,
in the middle of a Saturday. Once, she throws her rings into the sea.

In summer the zinnias bloom along the hillside while the baby
coos her animal song. *What is this life?* she thinks gaily. Still she
covers her motherhood like a scandal. Hushes it like a profanity.

For My Daughter on a Bad Day

Life will rough you up. Throw you to the
shore like a wave crashing—sand in your
hair, blood in your teeth. When grief sits
with you, hand dipped with rage, let it
linger. Hold its pulse in your hands. There
is no remedy for a bad haircut or ruined
love like *time*. Even when death is coming,
even when the filth rises in the back of
your throat—

this is not the worst of it. And if it is?
Listen for the catbird calling. No matter
the wreckage, they still sing for you.

Author's Note

The author wishes to express that this is a work of fiction. Names, characters, bodies, behaviors, and incidents in which men are rude or foul are either the product of the author's imagination or absolutely true. Any resemblance to actual persons, living or dead, or actual events is either purely coincidental or an act of deep-seated revenge. Further, this book is not intended as a substitute for medical, emotional, or spiritual advice. The reader should regularly consult their own inner voice in matters relating to his/her health and particularly with respect to any symptoms of lust, longing, and the desire to be free.

Acknowledgments

Thank you to Joanna MacKenzie for her tireless efforts and unwavering belief in my work. Without you, I would still be shouting into a bottomless void. Thank you to my incredible editor, Mary Gaule. You took a chance on this book and I'll be forever thankful for that. I'd also like to thank Joanne O'Neill for the gorgeous cover design as well as everyone else at Harper who made this possible, including Amanda Hong, Amy Baker, Emily VanDerwerken, and Lisa Erickson.

Thank you to the ever lovely Joanna Goddard who uses her platform to elevate female artists and writers who are finding their voice.

Thank you to my personal champions at home and online, especially those who have stuck with me through many first endeavours. Readers in their workplaces, school pick-up lines, and living rooms. I am so grateful for you.

Thank you to my parents and my sister who always believed this is where it was going to go.

Thank you to the women who have stood by me in every storm and sun: Carrie, Mo, Bethany, Heather, Natasha, Laura, Jenny, Liza, Rebecca, Katie, Tiffany, Jen, Lisa, Jess, Candis, and Elizabeth. When I write about friendship, I write about you.

Special thanks to Kayla and my mom who keep our children safe and happy while their parents work. Without you, this book would still be in its first draft.

Thank you to Ann Marie at the Panera in Hummelstown, Pennsylvania who made sure I sat in my booth with the outlet for my laptop so I could write this book. Your joy makes my day.

This book is dedicated to the teachers and professors who encouraged me from elementary school through my twenties to keep writing. The encouragement you give students to take risks and keep going is such important work.

Finally, unending love and gratitude to my husband and our children who show up on every page.

Acknowledgments

About the Author

Kate Baer is a #1 *New York Times* bestselling author and poet based on the East Coast of the United States. She has been featured in publications such as *Harper's Bazaar, Vogue.com, Entertainment Weekly & Literary Hub. What Kind Of Woman* is her first book.